Raptures of a
Rose

Raptures of a

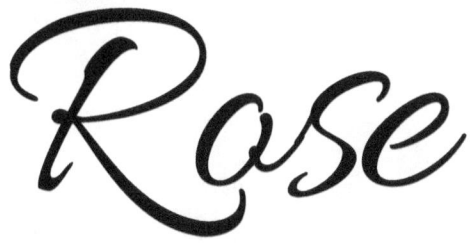
Rose

Rising is its Nature

USHA NANDIGAMA

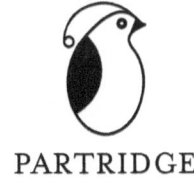

PARTRIDGE

To order additional copies of this book, contact
Partridge India
000 800 10062 62
orders.india@partridgepublishing.com

www.partridgepublishing.com/india

Contents

This book is dedicated to my Family

Prologue

Who Am I?

When the past haunts me and I am at Sea
Life poses a question which is always a mystery
Time & Again the question rises to erupt tranquillity
And for answer let me pose the question to you

Who Are You?

If neither your achievements nor your failures count,
Then how do you define yourself
If neither your heart nor your brain can gain a stand,
Then how do you identify yourself
If neither currency nor goods could carry value,
Then how do you recognize yourself
If neither flesh nor inhuman reflexes mean you,
Then how do you treat yourself
If neither Being Prey nor being the Predator suits you,
Then how do you assess yourself

I am neither the mountain carrying huge goodwill
Nor the Wind blowing at my own pace and will
I am neither the Sun that can shine Bright
Nor the Moon that can be soft and light
I am neither forest holding many mysteries in me
Nor the Desert open for the man to search and see
Then, Who Am I?

This book is part of the Quest.

Happy Reading!!!!!!!!!!!!!!!!!

A Page in the Book

Rise my dear from the current state
To surrender wilfully to the fate
Believing completely that the future
World Would be Yours to Nurture

Fate is the road for the brave to admire
Hope is the light that would always glimmer
Flowers and thorns teach myriad lessons
Filling the path with innocence and essence

Of expression & beliefs expressed in words
Ingrained stronger than stab of swords
Because sometimes it is must to be wound
To toughen up, stay awake & rebound

At times our vision is dizzy & blurred
everything seems to be twisted & twirled
The vision brings a sense of dizziness
The picture perfect state of weariness

You see yourself falling like a leaf
Questioning every source and belief
Wondering if every second is a pain
And the path itself is taken in vain

To believe that there shall be goodness
In even the vilest creature is not a weakness
It is a beautiful portrayal of your power
A strength that shall never ever hover

It is that vigour which shall enable you
To conquer the vile nature also in you
It shall gently replace the imperfections
With serene & fresh hopes & sensations

It shall refine you as an Angel on Earth
Striving for the good & with no dearth
Of unique & appreciable qualities
That shall enable you to grow your faculties

A hope that you can transform the wicked & mould
It is a belief in the ultimate goodness of the world
If you couldn't mould the vile & obnoxious
It is no failure of yours to become anxious

It is a humble attempt in striving for humility
For the ultimate goal of one's existence of humanity
Walking with head held high & upright
Towards the destiny's call in the guiding light

Take this moment to announce to yourself
That this is a walk to discover one's own self
Enjoy each & every awake moment of this ride
Holding your head high and heart with pride

This walk should not be referred to as a lost track
The pride in the walk is the gait not to attract
To display the power & strength of the ideals
Which one chooses without any bargain or deals

It is the power of the path that shall resound
and help human to be bound and rebound
This walk is a gentle one filled with humility
To reduce & put an end to all kinds of animosity

The walk is to signify co operation & coexistence
To collect a short & sweet memory from thence
To present it in a page in the book called life
To paint it beautifully & fill with delight in rife!

Torch of Humanity

Your gaze instils inspiration in me
To go ahead & reach far off land & see
Not just the wonders of the world
But also to gain self realization & hold
The pristine & glorious part of the soul
Unfazed in testing times & remain whole
To pass on the alight torch intact & not in parts
That is being carried in the heart of the hearts
The torch is a symbol of humanity
Blessed to all individuals with humility
The torch is the light that brightens
It is the light which enlightens
It is the dream, hope, guidance & passion
For which humanity is striving without cessation
Let me add some bright oil to the lamp
Let the torch burn bright for us to clamp
We are blessed to hold it for a while
Let us hold it with pride & walk a mile
When the moment comes to hand it over
Let us not fall prey for tactics or lower
The chance to hold the light & leave behind
It's a great gift to humanity to preserve & remind
The generations to come of the toil
Of their forefathers on this world's soil
Let us behold & beautify the passage with light
Fill the hearts of young lads with hope & might!

The Feeling of Being Reborn

The Phoenix wasted her pristine tears
with her foolishness & fears

That tore her apart & astray
She felt as if she was a prey

But realized at a fine moment
That there is no torment

More painful than being stuck
It is not by an element of luck

That she could cross this slay
But it is because of a ray

A ray that just guides all
It assures that you'll never fall

This ray brought her alive
As a new born to dive

The Changes within her terrified her
But also gave a chance to rise further

The fear inside stopped breathing
Giving a ray of hope to be glowing

To visit places of unknown heights
To see new & bright lights

Let this journey of the dove
Be full of amazement & Love

Let us all liberate our self
From the self created shelve

Let this dove be awakened
In all of us to be enlightened!

A Bride's Jitters

A beauty with no measure
A Love that is a treasure
Beaming with Pleasure
Yet Jitters in pressure

Travelling down the path of memory lane
Things of Past sounded too grand or lame
Yet few other times as mysteriously insane
And the future is both a boon and a bane

Though ancient, At times, the passage
took a new meaning seen from this stage
It has gained a new respect in today's age
But in life's course leaving a memorable page

Learnt from old faults & felt remorse
Learnt to bury the old fury for a new course
It is time to bury all of it to open new doors
It is that hour of the day to re-begin a new source

Leaning back to the past teaches remorse
lets us to bury the pain and open new doors
To learn and unlearn a novel lovely course
For the memories are life's best resource

With this acceptance she moved towards the aisle
Leaving the best man and smiling from her viel
But the heart is slowly recovering from the hustle
To open a new door keeping away all past tussle

The new door is attractive & appears bright
Filling her heart with new hope and great insight
Bathing her and her beau with an unknown light
Making every step worthwhile in this wait.

A Jade Vine

The flower that grew an extra mile
To bring back a long lost smile

Taking off your breath for a while
Is called a beautiful Jade Vine

The beauty of a passing water flow
With a pace that is sweet and slow

Captured in an immobilized glow
To rise a new vision from low

You could feel the warm breeze
Gently removing all the crease

Feeling afresh and anew with peace
There is an unknown ease

An orb guided us to her place
The path to there sans any race

Her inner beauty increased her grace
It gently lit brightly all the ways

All the days of the beautiful flower are now
Full of surprises, newness and love

Her heart & actions are as pure as a dove
Making her the most beautiful Frau

Everyone is given a chance to choose
This is the time to be diligent & muse

Life is not meant to be an unworthy ruse
So tells that flower that challenges our views

When the choices are made in spirit
It shall be followed by truth and merit

The path for every nugget is also lit
It is a decision of the heart and wit

A portrait

A dream like view in the eyes
Looking above at the skies

Glowing & enchantingly nice
An expression that can stab vice

A thought provoking gait
Unique combination of mercy & might

Self absorbed at any new sight
A presence blessed after a long wait

A smile that can rob away all pain
It can cure even the stab or slain

A memory that can never ever wane
A treasure of hope that makes one sane

A portrayal that reminds one's purpose
A tale that reminds there's nothing to lose

The human birth is for a noble cause
Each moment is the result of what we chose

Cloak

The darkness around was very scary
It took without any warning away all the merry
The insides slowly started feeling wary
Suffocated as if buried deep in a quarry

It looked as if wrapped completely tight
In a cloak without any sense of wrong or right
Everything appeared blurred and lost sight
Lost track of time & endured a long wait

The darkness covering inside the cloak
Began drinking deep the soul & soak
It was quite heavy just like a rock
After a while experienced a gentle knock

The knock shook away all the barriers
It was from the Angels who are the carriers
Of Hope and rebirth to all the warriors
To remind the true nature to the saviours

Woke up with an unknown yet gentle force
Started searching the reason & the source
For the self created cloak & it's hoarse
Impact on the gentle and warm course

Accepted that there were layers of fears
It's not a cloak but fears hoarded over years
Fear is eating away all strength creating smears
It's time to break the shell & follow the path of seers

Picked up courage to fight back all fear
To again become closer to all the dear
To come closer to true self & near
To the life's ultimate goal & be crystal clear

The cloak is destroyed just by this first stride
Became feather light and placidly drifted for a ride
Slowly but serenely in the chosen path of drive
It is like breathing fresh air & feeling alive

Your depiction

My path seemed rough & full of plight
I lost all glow, confidence & might
Suddenly my eyes deviated to a new sight
For a second there was calmness in my fights

I regained composure slowly to look ahead
Inner voices told me that I'm alive not yet dead
I took the first step crushing the entire weed
My path became clear & then is sown a new seed

When my concentration was on the path
Nothing exceptional happened except wrath
But the moment I've felt you & subsided all math
It seemed amusingly fresh as if a divine bath

Now my path and the steps are for you
There is no pristine gift in life except your view
Not anymore lost in dark or feeling rue
I rejoice the time spent in recollecting you

I cannot depict your valour in paint
I cannot describe your stride as I'm no saint
I've felt fresh breeze & so trying to mount
To feel you on a future date, without any count

Slow steps towards you have taught me silence
I've learnt important lessons like resilience
Now you are the path that I wish to walk in diligence
There is no force that can cause severance

With all this enchantment, muse & beauty in the passage
I shall carry your impressions as a Universal message
I cannot describe you in a phrase as I'm still a savage
To depict you one has to transform from a savage to a sage

Scars speaking

I may appear to be a mystical mystery
Yet this is not a new rhyme in history

You may perceive me to be a challenge
But the glory shall be in the avenge
This is not a tale of revenge
And surely not to derange

The wound was imprinted in momentary passion
Bearing the scar is to depict compassion
The Healing taught me unknown sensation
Letting me feel the very Divine Depiction

The vile needs to get up from the snore
We are born to be united not to deplore
Life is an enchanting expedition to explore
It is an opportunity to open a new door

You may take me as a puzzle
But I'm not meant to dazzle
I shall not stay to create hassle
I shall try & put an end to a tussle

You can neither possess me
Nor can you control me
You can neither comprehend me
Nor can you define yourself to me

This journey started as a joyful ride
It had many twists & turns in the stride
Your unspoken grief remained safe in my hide
I tried to bury all rivalry and be your confide

In return for the scars imprinted on me by you
I shall leave a mark of compassion for you
Which shall always remind you my presence
Though I shall always be a mystery in your essence

I may appear to be a mystical mystery
Yet this is not a new rhyme in history

Your Abode

I shall come to your abode with reverence
Bow in front of the altar with sober sense

I shall join my hands in your prayer
To guide me forever without any waver

It is my nature that wavers & drifts
Yet I pray you to guide me in all rifts

I solemnly pray to be the light
So that I shall be filled with might

Words cannot be joined to describe
The gracious adoration of your vibe

Forgive my prattle and confusion
Guide me to bring synergetic fusion

Let me re-begin as a new born pristine flower
After I bow humbly in front of your Divine shower!

A Fighter- my rider

I was entangled in a dark place in my dream
Presumed this to be the reality of my realm
Was scary, this is the untoward end it had seem
I was unknown & strange; a ghost to myself I deem

Blindly believed that there is no more air
Suffocation strained me & felt lost in this fair
The darkness covering me is difficult to wear
I wish to discard it & move fast like a mare

The body became slowly lighter and lighter
From far off saw an armour clad fighter
There is nothing in life to detest or deter
The pain inside has slowly made me mightier

I know the fighter from unknown past & age
The fighter had the calmness of a sage
The armour is to wage a war against the rage
It is to break free from shackles or any cage

Fresh dawn is welcoming & I slowly realized
That it was just a strange dream that seized
All the reality away & my breath almost ceased
My new dawn woke me & I felt delighted

The fighter is the rider of my new dawn
I felt slow growth inside me as if a fawn
Followed the halo that encircled the lawn
My faith in you shall not make me feel worn

Dark deeds need not be sent to the jury
A confession with the rider removes all weary
My fighter and rider is the hope that can bury
Any kind of evil intentions or destroy fury

A mysterious chamber

I have a heart that solemnly sings
Cherishes when timeless truth rings
Wishes to fly high and wide with wings
Beats every moment for the unknown & blinks

It is described as fragile by the world around
I feel it is my pride that which can surround
My very subtle existence, yet feels bound
To the myriad ways of life, waiting to be found

My heart is a mystery that may not be unveiled
Yet the goal is not to find a way or to yield
But to leave a mark on this fertile field
To leave a legacy ahead and not to wield

Many a wars are fought in this chamber
It tries to establish peace & destroy danger
Has been the war field where the foe is anger
Always a fresh foot has been put forward to clamber

My heart is a pristine dew drop in the ocean
A combination of many feelings to form a potion
Has many curious views and a clinging question
For its Creator to answer & give His decision!

Your Presence

Glory that no ordinary being can paint
Beauty that no foe can ever try to taint
Presence resembling a divine saint
A portrait that brings faith in the heart of the faint

Your presence is a divine gift
To cross all pain & any kind of rift
To walk towards the goal in a swift
To stay serene & add meaning to the drift

You are the unknown which my heart tries to find
You are the all known truth that can flow with wind
You are the protector, rider and the hope to mankind
Yet you are the mystery that cannot be described by mind

I've tried describing you to the world in my words
But it was a fruitless attempt and replied by swords
Swords not made of iron or steel but that rung chords
Yet I start your story of glory in new tones & wards

A blanket of illusion is too tightly wrapped on our eyes
We are not able to see the reality and rise above the skies
We are tied up in petty battles of ego and vies
It's time to discover the real identity and reach new highs

Moment differences cease, your glory will be in invincible paint
There shall be no foe who intends to destroy your beauty or taint
We shall worship in unison your Presence as a divine saint
As your portrait brings faith even in the heart of the faint

To a Long Lost Friend

I've waited for you, my dear long lost friend
You couldn't recognize me, so would like to send
A message; before parting ways, that life is not an end
This is the time that shall not come again to mend

The ways chosen in one's own path
Mark the journey's essence not its wrath
It's a place to learn & grow like a heath
Vengeance leads not to any powerful seat

Ways chosen mark the fulfilment of gratification
Few ways fill one with strange & serene sensation
But yet all this land's ways are an illusion
My prayer for you is not to get lost in this delusion

One's journey is marked with choices anew
The beauty is to capture the moment in its view
Greed leaves one in a state of confusion & rue
The purpose is not to accumulate but be like dew

Dew drop in the ocean of human compassion
A blooming bud in the field of your passion
Not to be the initiator of any sort of aversion
Let your way lead you & not turn into a diversion

Innumerable times bestowed with His grace
This is the time to identify your race
Not to climb someone else's tower in haze
Sans illusion this world shall no more be a maze

I've come to spend some time with my old friend
But realized lately that there is nothing I can lend
As it might turn to be a meeting with a conflicting end
Let me not see an uneventful end so I leave you to mend

I shall carry with me only the memories of good old days
All the haze and pain in between shall be burnt in the rays
The rays of my new journey ahead with its fresh ways
To forget and forgive myself; to lighten for all the old plays

Light & Bird

Hope is the light that can be lit even in a dark alley
Faith is the bird that can sing even in melancholy

Let us light the candle of hope in our heart
Let the bird of faith sing to re-create our art

Let us take a step forward & rise after calamity
To learn & breathe in fresh essence to humanity

Let us pledge to carry forward the torch of light
Let this sojourn be filled with pride and no fight

Let the bird sing the unsung song of our soul till the destiny
Let the light enlighten us to spread this message till infinity

Christmas Gift

A story that has no beginning or end
That which resonates to serenely send

A universal message and a truth
The acceptance of which bears a fruit

A present not made of any precious metal
But it is the realization of divine detail

The reason for the present day events
That mystically erases the entire past vents

It is a lesson which humans are aware
Since ages but at times do not care

Seers call it Unconditional love
That bounds none & frees the dove

The dove of joy and calmness inside us
It radiates those around without fuss

The divine call that makes duty
As sweet as honey till we reach infinity

This song of the human soul's connections
Is not to be lost for vile & petty intentions

Many a time lost in the worldly chatter & races
I forget this message passed across human races

Your presence resonates graciously this message
It is passed by you humbly & subtly just as a sage

I can neither define if you are a poet or a philosopher
Nor can I paint & describe you as a saviour or warrior

Yet my soul awakens to your presence
You are the nectar that fills life's essence

You are the hope that can enlighten my life's ill-lit passages
You are the faith, which makes me memorize your messages

I have awakened to your presence, it's my Christmas morning
A divine dawn; from then I'm filled forever with your adoring

You are the wrapped Christmas morning gift
That which removes in a swift way any kind of rift

I've re-discovered myself in your gentle & gracious gaze
Your eyes radiate this Universal message in beautiful rays

Lanes and By-lanes in the Journey

Unique combination of meditative lanes
Acquaintances and strangers meet across these by-lanes
Winds blow along with us in these mysterious lanes
Few winds carry rhythmic patterns and fill the strange lanes
The winds pass away but its musings are absorbed by the historic lanes
These vibrations leave an intangible mark on the Wonderful Lanes

Foot prints in these lanes at times create History
At other times they remain a mystery
These lanes are filled with Eccentricity
There is a presence of Divine Felicity
But the appealing aspect is the Serenity
That keeps one moving is searching for one's own Destiny.....

What shall we name these lanes?
A journey called Life or a passage in the process of Transformation?
Whatever, be it named...

It is a Progressive Journey filled with amusement
Leaving you in a state of mystifying enchantment.

Inner Chatter to Abound

The moment the inner chatter would just halt
Your Brain would just have nothing to fault

That moment when the heart embraces solace
When a naked eye catches a glimpse of divine plays

Then the human heart begins its onward voyage
One experiences the calmness of a sage

There is a synchrony set in this path
For the destiny of the journey is not yet dealt

The beauty of the voyage makes you spell bound
With no choice but to remain mystically abound!

Maze & Its Presence

I entered a mysterious maze
Where in I could not gaze

Too many things captured my attention
Slowly I got lost in this sensation

By the time I recovered, it is dusk
My heart beat fast & sank in the dust

Soon I fell into a deep slumber
My sleep was full of encumber

I woke up to see another dawn
And felt gentle like a swan

Then began my quest
Filled with unique jest

This is my expedition's essence
The reason for the maze's presence...

Good Morning - Breeze

When the fresh morning breeze touches your forehead
There are many wonderful expressions flowing unsaid

Those expressions which are carried by the birds
Expressions which cannot be described in words

But these beautiful impressions are carried day long
Messages flow deep into your heart like an unsung song

It is life's humming to fill one with just and might
To rejuvenate each day with fresh and glowing light!

Fairy Inside You

Just like the monsoon's first showers
The heart is filled with fresh powers

Infinite though invisible to the world around
A sense of tranquillity to those who surround

Just like the warmth of mother's love
As white and as pure as a dove

Professing an undeniable charisma
Filled with an unspeakable enigma

It is like waking up from a deep sleep
Peeping at the one's own self deep

It is discovering a new you
That which seems strangely untrue

For truth or untruth doesn't hold
Imperative is to stay tight & let it unfold

As it may seem soothing or scary
For the process is to find a Fairy

A Fairy tale of Self discovery
Just like a Treasure's Re-discovery!

Christmas Morning

You are my life's Christmas Morning
Filled each moment with gracious adorning

You came without an invitation
But filled me with a mystical sensation

It is indeed a pleasant surprise
Along with the morning sunrise

Your arrival is marked with newness
Helping me to improve my keenness

You taught me to pay attention
As each moment in life has an intention

Each moment is a treasure
Beyond quantitative measure

But my life's greatest treasure is you
Without which everything seems rue

Every moment I feel your presence
Makes me realize my life's essence

Unknowingly I've been waiting for your embrace
You presented yourself majestically with Grace

Just like the Christmas Morning
My heart is in a deep trance of adoring....

Rising Phoenix

You feel Divine Angels speaking
Opening new channels of thinking

There is a sense of twinkling
Your eyes are miraculously shining

Your entire frame is rising
It is a sign of a journey's beginning

You can feel messages flowing
At times it seems time is freezing

This is living life with a meaning
Just like a phoenix rising!

Mystical Wand

At times I'm stuck for right choice of words
Wandering like a ghost in this forest of swords.

At other times my words flow without interruption
These expressions may seem to the world as disruption.

Slowly it became imperative to learn to be silent
This beautiful lesson has made me resilient.

There is an inner beauty in silence
Teaching the quality of self reliance.

Deep inside you there is a Wonderland
Opened only with a mystical wand.

This mystical wand can be termed as Peace
To cast its magic the external turmoil must cease!

Miles to reach for Your brilliance

I've walked virtually miles
To experience Your divine smiles

The smile which robs away pain
Fills one with an unknown gain

The moment I heard Your mirth
It was no less than rebirth

Being re-born from my own ashes
I almost forgot everything except for few flashes

These flashes include your warmth & gentleness
This filled my mysterious journey with cheerfulness

This journey taught me perseverance
I'm lost for words in your reverence

The day I meet You again
I hope to recount Your reign

Till I bid adieu to this world & existence
Let me stay warm in Your grace & brilliance!

Sea shore walk

On a breezy morning I walked towards the shore
As the pristine waters were inspiring my heart's core

The rising waters had a strange serenity
The excellence which connects you to infinity

The falling waters displayed mysterious melancholy
That which curiously converted into a melody

The gentle water that washed your feet
Is like a good old friend's greet

It washes away all your pain
You are now an Angel without any feign

This friend understands your feelings
Without your lips opening its sealing's

It is then you start playing like a kid
Without realizing the magic the water did

Rising and falling waters profess deeper meaning
Making you add sense to your wakeful dreaming

The Angel in you now radiates with brilliance
The calmness at the shore makes you exemplify excellence

You pocket the rare gifts brought by your friend
These shells & memories shall be till the end

You love to stay in this dreamily awake state forever
But there are other aspects demanding your endeavour

So, hastily just like you I had to bid farewell
But the Angel in me and my friend's gifts shall dwell!

The call

The birds were humming in chorus
The wind was blowing with full force
The sun is peeping through the sky and mountains
The water is gushing like the fountains

The earth's surface is warm and soothing
As there is a fire like truth burning
In the lap of the nature I hear a calling
Voice so familiar yet alien like a saying

"Open your compassionate heart and mind
These are the gifts of being born in this land
Experience each & every second
As it is the 'present' in your hand

Each and every moment has a message
That which liberates you from cage
The cage that which you've built
Out of ignorance and guilt

Break these shackles and walk a mile
The destiny comes closer without any vile
Present yourself as a mighty warrior
At the same time, be a peace maker and saviour

Burn the myths and superstitions
For life is not a cruel abolition
Live life to the fullest in times of pain and gain
Make an undeniable mark before your footprints wane

Leave a legacy for your grand children to learn & hear
Let them grow to be divine Angels without fear
Live each and every second
As it is the 'present' in your hand!"

In the lap of the nature's five elements
This message is one of the Supreme presents
Simple and subtle truth known since ages
The essence of human existence, so say the sages.

Our search

Each time the passing wind whispers in your ears
Be enlightened and carry no grudges or fears;

The running water that has no destined flow
Teaches to keep moving and let go;

The clear and cloudy skies
Shows that there are lows and highs;

The warmth of the Mother earth
To remember our blessed birth;

Burning fire reminds that the passions
Have to be fulfilled in right assertions;

Each passing moment reminds you dear
The purpose is to learn and share here;

As nothing is permanent in this land
Until we breathe our last on this sand;

Then why do we keep searching for permanency
In this ever changing planet of Supremacy/ Excellency?

Notably Simple Existence-
Simple or Complicated?

The joy in a child's innocent & simple ways
The warmth in the early morning sunrays

Beauty of the blue sky just before the rain
That washes away all the heart's deep pain

Freshly blossomed flowers fragrance
Which fills one's heart with heavenly essence

Simple and innocent gifts of this planet add colour
To move forward in this gifted world with valour

At times we destroy this beauty in the name of war
Filling our hearts with deep wounds and roar

At times it is filled with unrequited differences
That creates artificial boundaries & appearances

Did we complicate our gifted simple life in this Garden?
Leaving ourselves miserably without any pardon?

It is no time to blame ourselves or punish
We didn't arrive on this garden to banish

Let's make our existence notably simple
And make this Divine garden a Temple

Simple life with meaning and essence
Each moment shall be a delightful presence!

Gifts in fists

Each one of us carried beautiful gifts
In our tiny & delicate closed fists

The moment we were born here
We agreed to share them & learn

As our flesh started growing stronger
We didn't bother about the deal any longer

At times we forgot the gifts bestowed
Made our lives thorny and skewed

Any road taken leads us to our destiny
But thorny paths make us loose clarity

Always a time comes to open our fists
With no choice but to distribute the gifts

Then, why do we have to wait for a time
As though benefaction is a crime

These gifts aren't man-made
We carried them to serve as an aide

Brought these presents from far off places
Significance of which is forgotten in the races

Any chosen path can be filled with joy
Provided we wilfully share and enjoy

There is nothing like a thorny or well laid path
It's a choice in our hands to lead it sans wrath

To open our hands & start distribution
For creation starts with contribution

Thorny path changes to a garden of roses
Once our innate nature unveils itself & discloses.

Freedom

There's light inside each person's heart
It is indeed a wonderful piece of art

It can cast away all fears and darkness
Fill one with illumination and brightness

This piece of art is secured with a key
That which opens when you are not 'at sea'

The secret to use the key is to be liberated
Without any prejudices and be enlightened!

Shields that none can wield

Deep inside the heart are buried unfathomable wounds
Difficult to be expressed in words or sounds
Memories at times make these wounds appear fresh
Draining inner energies & creating virtual pain in flesh
These wounds are severe than a sword's slain
Worst part is the revisiting of these memoires & pain.

You intend to destroy it with a sword
So that you can feel calm, safe & restored
But this process paradoxically causes intense loss
Your heart bleeds profusely & you are at cross
Soothing balm is imperative for such healing
Time is an aid in such a deep wound's sealing

Should one wait for the right time & feel torn?
Distastefully bear the pain & feel worn?
Can't it be cast off & one stay composed?
Yes, of course the pain was never imposed
Indeed, it was your choice to expose your heart
It's in your hands to stop playing a victim's part.

Time or destiny is never so harsh or cruel
Time presents itself beautifully like a jewel
Jewels for which you cannot repay
That which no sword or dagger can slay
It is noble to choose the ideal of forbearance
Do not retort to the path of vengeance.

For Darkness can never ever conquer light
Dark scars can be combated only with a tough fight
Forbearance and compassion spread light

Filling your heart with mystical might
Making you mysteriously feather like
One gets a chance to have life's hike.

Deep scars are indeed gifts in disguise
They advise the sleeping soul to arise
Fresh powers are found in bountiful
Rejuvenating life & making it colourful
Forbearance, compassion are life's greatest treasures
Preparing you to combat beyond any measures.

They are your protectors and act as a shield
No trespasser can never ever dream to wield
You are prepared now to erase not only scars
But you are ready for any sort of wars
For the biggest enemies is our inner qualm
And you've learnt to rest them and stay calm!

Guide or a Valkyrie or a Fairy?

First time when I saw your reflection
I was lost for words & filled with affection

It was like drenching one's deep thirst
Who was wandering in an unknown quest

I was lost and searching for my path
When you courteously reminded my worth

Wondered, if I was looking at my own image
Your eyes reflected the calmness of a sage

I re-discovered myself in your tender beam
Your appearance is a divine presence in any realm

It seems as though it is just now, that we met
But unable to grasp and tell who you are yet

You could be a Valkyrie or a Fairy or a Guide
To imbibe fresh energy and muse in my ride!

Tower of Power

Two lone travellers began a quest
One of them started from the west
The other's home is in the east
Their journey is a crucial test
Their destiny is in the north
They should keep moving forth
Not just any but a very high tower
In the north which is a symbol of power
Is presumed to be their journey's end
Perseverance is vital for them to transcend.

The day they met each other they were strangers
Together they walked miles & cast away dangers
Though the lone travellers were nomads
As time passed they turned to be comrades
They shared each other's pain and gain
Learnt many a lessons in this campaign
They cherished each other's company
Their differences turned to be a symphony
They grew matured and wise in this journey
Relished each and every moment without hurry.

Their onward journey is filled with many a miracle
Not with a wild passion to reach the pinnacle
Yes, they did reach their tower on a fine morning
The tower was magnificently charming
But what filled their heart with contentment & happiness
Was the lovely journey that removed all their emptiness
This is the beautiful voyage of east and west
It is stride of tolerance without any rest
To reach the high tower in the extreme the north
To learn and spread knowledge, which is of immense worth.

Stranger in a Familiar Path

During a usual evening stroll
To pass on fresh energy to the soul

A little girl came across an Angel
The girl thought her to be a stranger

But realized the creature has wings
And glides gracefully like swans

The girl started a chat with this celestial Damsel
The girl believed her abode to be a far off castle

The girl asked about the angel's home
Is it Himalayas or Tokyo or London or Rome?

The angel smiled and replied splendidly
That her existence is heavenly

And she is not born into any castle
That her home is a heart free of hassle

The girl enquired when she can meet her again
Reply is; angel is present where ever goodness reigns

And that she is present inside each one of us
One needs to be empathetic to see her, thus!

Destined Walk

The day a baby is born & opens its tender eyes
Parents and acquaints celebrate with great joys

As the child grows and learns about the world
Many strange and paradoxical views unfold

Morals teach you to love your neighbour
And be affectionate and be a saviour

In reality to survive in this mysterious web
To reach your goal you shouldn't miss a step

Steps to your goal include being self centric
But this quality at times makes you eccentric

That is the reason we were taught quite early
To be compassionate and respond fairly

The grown up kid is split for choice
Lost in this complex web without a voice

Clarity is born out of confusion
This is reality and not an illusion

It is imperative to take a middle path
Loving and being kind without earning any wrath

Walk with your companions in greater truths' find
Life's purpose is in greater good of mankind.

Rediscovery

The magnificence of getting lost
Is generally not appreciated by most

Too much concentration on the goal
Makes you worry about your role

But, your role is to enjoy the serenity around
And the beautiful musings that surround

To listen and imbibe each moment's message
Develop the compassion & tolerance of a sage

When your 'self' leaves you and wanders around
Then only is the beauty deep inside you found

You start understanding and correlating
That the process of creation & destruction is on-going

All differences are superficial and an illusion
Unity is the universally acclaimed solution

This is the beauty of getting lost & your discovery
It leads to a simple and profound truth's re-discovery.

Home

The place where you feel cosy
It might not be very grand or rosy
It is a lovely place called the home
Wherein your thoughts never roam
Your soul is filled with mirth & never alone
There's someone to understand your moan
You have the company of a shoulder to lean
That support which will never wane
Your bliss and ache can be shared
Without an element of being feared

You are never judged based on your choices
Your deep rooted ideas find their voices
At a place where your success is rejoiced
Fears in the moment of failure are destroyed
Your deep wounds are nursed
Unknowingly, you learn to be immersed
Immersed in the appreciation of their beauty
And you assume to protect it as your duty
Slowly you turn to be a warrior
You are advised to be a saviour

Saviour not for your home, but the world at large
To be a defender & gracefully emerge
So where is this place called home?
Is it a city or a mansion or just a dome?
Home is a place where you discover yourself
It is a mirror which reflects your divine self
It may be a person or a message
That which takes away all rage
That which teaches you to be in harmony
There is divinity & peace in this synchrony.

Capture to Enrapture

Objects that shine mystically
Adding untold grace wilfully

Windows for unspoken emotions
That which are deeper than oceans

They mirror your own reflection
There is no place for any imperfection

Beautifully carved and painted
With a message to be untainted

Their messages never deceive one
Through which Hearts can be won

Carefully designed by divinity
Presented as a gift to humanity

Expression is its untaught gift
That can drive away any rift

Can capture any of the life's moment
To preserve safely forever in contentment

Can express pain very naturally
Without uttering a word verbally

They can drive away any sort of fear
Expressing that you are very Dear

Battles and differences can be put to an end
Best wishes can be sent to your friend

They are the windows of the soul
The expression of which makes one whole.

Eyes can talk, smile and remain enraptured
The whole universe's expression can be captured.

Flow of wind

The Moving Wind had no set direction
Yet filled heart with a strange sensation

Then The Flow moves towards a rift
In a manner which is simply swift

Diminishing the Feel that it is controlled
You realise the flow has completely changed

Now you acknowledge and start to comprehend
That there is no reason to control or apprehend

The beauty is to let the serenity flow
In this process you can simply grow.

Battle

Winning the battles gives one glory
Your fame spreads like a legendary story

People bow to your wishes and will
But there is something you miss still

There is always an inner battle inside
You are unable to take sides or decide

You can feel divided into many parts
They are the broken pieces of your heart

To re-join them you need not win
Nor commit any blunder or sin

Paradoxically at times you should lose
It's only then that healing of bruises

Starts without application of any lotion
This in itself is the miraculous solution

It is only if we lose to great powers
That we shall experience Divine Showers...

Milestones or Just Miles and Stones

A traveller began a journey of milestones
Collected as many as possible gemstones

Precious blue stones that never fade
Proud of the mementos that never shade

Pocketed them safely in various decks
To ensure they are not lost in wrecks

Pile of his collections multiplied day by day
Started assuming that these stones have a way

To achieve anything and everything in life
Entered into innumerable number of strife

Because his confidence was his precious pebbles
In this process he earned many a rebels

Rebels who disliked not his collection
But they despised his reflection

As time passed the traveller was left
With a lot of enemies and scared of theft

He spent his retirement protecting his treasure
Evading his sleep and forgetting leisure

At last on a sleepless night
He had a terrible fight

His heart questioned his very existence
The purpose of his prolonged persistence

Searching for the answer in a gloomy mansion
He had a painful stroke and lost expansion

His dying moment's pain was behind comprehension
Left his enemies and rebels in a state of apprehension

The traveller's soul couldn't rest in peace
The inner war which he began didn't cease

Society decided to pass on this story to their progeny
To ensure peaceful co existence & homogeneity

Let no man shall die such a lonely and painful death
For that co-existence should be filled in each breath.

From Who to How

Words which need not be written
Assurances that need not be given

Trust that never wavers
Without expecting any favours

Passion that never dies
Humility that never flies

Acceptance which is inborn
Feelings that need not be sworn

Pain and pleasure go hand in hand
It is not just a mystical wand

Promises that need not be spelt out
Any difference can be ironed out

Indeed a strange unknown feeling
Words cannot describe this dealing

Time cannot measure this affection
One can see their own reflection

In this journey of paradoxes
They can be said to phalanxes

They are together even in separation
Can stay knit well even in abjection

Unique bond of sharing between these souls
Cannot be described in terms of any goals

Because the ultimate goal is greater good
This contribution cannot be understood

It is difficult to define who these souls are
Or from where they are or why they are

They are on a purpose and a mission
They shall beautifully weave the vision

A dream these comrades alone can express
To make it a reality for the world's progress

So, vital is not who or what or why they are here
But how they make this world a better sphere

This story is cherished and re-told even in a tide
In admiration and memory of their divine stride.

Protector

You are my protector
You are my defender

You wage battles for me
Without even seeing me

Silently bearing all pain to make my life
Always ready to walk even on a knife

You do not set limitations
Nor have any expectations

You are ready to cross the devil or sea
Just to assure that all is well for me

I cannot return or repay your debt
I will always accompany you in the path set

I can say I shall stay with you
For life for me means you

I've lost & rediscovered myself
In the reflection which is thyself

There is nothing like 'me' left now
What is left is an unbreakable vow

A vow where in, forever is a beginning
As this is the start of our meaningful living.

Journey of Gems Discovery

It is beautiful to get lost
You may find dew or frost
There is serenity if one wanders
Can't be achieved if one surrenders

Wander till that date and time
When you yourself feel a chime
With your heart and the surrounding
You offer yourself to this astounding

You re-discover your lost spark
And thus leave a permanent mark
Do not tie your ankles till that moment
As re-discovery is no less than atonement

Don't bury yourself in shackles
Confusions are like jackals
Don't surrender yourself to that suffocates
You are not here to obey parasites

Let your breath and thought flow
Free from any interruption like a glow
Don't harm yourself or your companions
For in this trip you may discover canyons

Great canyons of deeper insights and meanings
It is for you to understand these feelings
Do not interpret or judge them
Because your mission is to discover a gem

A gem buried deep inside you
That which resonates denoting true
A universal truth for which seers
Might have spent literally years

You appear gracious in this trip
You might find predators who try to rip
Parasites who repeatedly like to sip
Do not be cruel or use your whip

It is not your job to punish
You didn't come to banish
You are always on a way to vanish
In this short meeting try to cherish

Do not carry grudges or burden
Do not destroy the peace in the garden
Do the best you can for them
Never create any mayhem

Let go and move forward graciously
Don't depict yourself ostentatiously
Take simple strides away from these problems
In your journey of self-discovery of gems.

Tracks- Power of love or Love for power

Remove the illusions covering your eyes
All the delusions surrounding naturally dies

Try to see the world with wipe open eyes
Just like a curious little kid & be wise

For the world is an ever changing game
The blue print of which is not in fame

Rules of this game are no where defined
But you are always given a choice to be refined

The power of love or love for power
Can be determined in each & every hour

It is your choices that define you as a person
For, ultimate truth can't be an imitation version

Before you get ready and buckle up your shoes
Just be sure about the race track you choose

As this is your game, you may change the track
But that moment you shouldn't turn blank

You need to have the courage to restart
There is an unusual beauty in playing this part

You are never too old or too young to begin
When you restart your heart is contended within

As it's your heart beat that you are following now
You tend to admire everything and stay in love

The previously difficult experiences now seem
To be your passing friends and you beam

You are not scared but at peace this time
Because you are not entirely after dime

Eventually you shall arrive at your destiny
It remains a very well discovered mystery

It shall be more than your expectations
Filling you in strange revelations

But, keep moving with wide open eyes
For the limit is beyond the blue skies

There are no limits to these highs
So keep moving gently and be wise!

Nobility

The moment you lose your persistence
Slowly start questioning your very existence

When you try to comprehend life's essence
Get lost in self created destructive fences

Grope for light in pitch dark room
Scared deep inside that you may doom

You touch upon a burning candle
It creates a bruise that you can't handle

Not that the injury is so intense or deep
But lately you are habituated to weep

On trivial and illogical issues & things
Building myriad fences and rings

Break the self created ring or barrier
Awake to the fact that you are a warrior

Try to carry the candle's light
With the poise to win and fight

Your foes are the self created limitations
Remember you need not reach any expectations

If you follow the light and spread it
You cross all expectations & can lit

A spark called happiness and hope
In many a lives beyond imagination's scope

You shall have a place in their heart forever
Your fame & nobility is like a flowing river.

Burdens

There are times when we feel heavy
Ability to concentrate appears wavy

Not able to arrive at conclusions
Perplexed with strange delusions

Intend to cast off all the burdens
Would like to rush & cross these hurdles

But the reality is one cannot run away
From the past deeds or the present day

One feels fear gripping and choked
One's own self is ridiculed and mocked

This is not mockery of life's situation
But a beautiful way of insulation

One feels burdened or heavy
When one is not yet completely ready

To accept a simple but strange truth
This not an end, but it is a feeling of Ruth

One needs to cast off the excessive baggage
This is what is causing all the damage

Baggage includes those which you collected
But never belonged to you, if you had reflected

So all this worries and confusions
Are indeed the very solutions

Cast off few burdens just like jetsam
Don't feel heavy this is not an exam

You are just redistributing the things
This enables you to have new wings

You are ready to fly to new shores
Explore and extract new ores

These ores are not just for you
Look at them from a different view

Do not commit the same old mistake
But cherish the gifts and awake

To the valuable secret that there is nobility
In sharing, this is in fact your responsibility.

Despair

In the moments of distress and despair
When your heart's pain is beyond repair

At the times when storms hit you strong
You are unable to decide right or wrong

You are immersed in a sea of turmoil
Filled in trance like state of surreal

Everything around you appears like a passing
Your heart and brain's thoughts are racing

Your voice starts becoming feeble
But your insides would like to rebel

This is a moment of tough fight
It is not a moment to pause or wait

Be brave, the world is for you to walk
Neither you nor anyone has a right to mock

Walk in silence but with firm steps
Each step should show your depths

It should echo your convictions
You are ready to fight any addictions

This is the moment to make a choice
To choose the easy path or your inner voice

Your inner voice guides you only till that day
When you're ready to fight anything on your way

You're new born steps should firmly resound
The pain that you've undergone & rebound

This is in itself a message to you & everyone
Life is for happy communion and not to run

Let's pass on this simple message to all
So that our progeny don't degrade or fall.

Rebuilt Nest

All our life we are busy building
What we term as a cosy nesting

We pick things from the surrounding
Pile them in a way that is astounding

We accumulate things randomly
Assuming this as our duty solemnly

In our hurry to build the nest
We laid many a things to rest

At times hurt others in our pre-occupation
Acquaintances assumed it as exploitation

We have built our home near a sea
On a very big and beautiful tree

So that fresh air shall pay a visit
And keeps us alive and exquisite

We assumed our nest to be bullet proof
Ignorantly blissful days spent under the roof

A day came when our little nest
Could not stand a unique test

It broke into pieces because of the water
Rising water brought all the slaughter

Our nest was very close to the sea
For that reason couldn't be damage free

Other birds instead of consoling us
Chose to make a big unnecessary fuss

Instead of helping to rebuild the nest
And calming down and giving rest

Agitated our spirit and created mess
We decided to rebuild & not to stress

This is the beauty & courage to rebuild
To fill one with fresh powers & be thrilled

This time our simple & new nest is not
Bullet proof, as this is not we sought

But our hearts have become strong
Resilient all through the journey long.

Serene Abode

Distant from the hustle and bustle
Quite far away from all sort of tussle

There is a serene and lovely place
Where there is no need to be in race

You are at liberty to express your views
Emote & share all mews and news

Free from all kinds of judgement
You are at liberty to experiment

There is no failure or success here
Everything is a lesson there

Every human enters as a student
With questions & who is prudent

There is no need to exit this abode
It is like a journey on a road

Where there is no beginning or end
Mesmerizing events on the road send

Great message across to the world
You are gifted a chance to mould

Both one's own & others' lives
One is filled with liveliness and dives

Deep into a world filled with light
You are now armour less knight

There is no need to grope in darkness
To arrive at this mystical brightness

This is your open heart & awakened soul
That can make everything feel whole.

Prayer

Each time I'd like to recollect your presence
I gaze at the sky to absorb your essence

What I absorb is a wonderful celestial joy
That makes me immune to all kinds of ploy

Strange ploys which humans enact
It is better for anyone not to react

For these are weird human acts
That which at times are beyond facts

Without your encouraging smile
My whole life may become vile

You give me strength and energy
Not to fight but to create synergy

But at times my vision becomes blurred
My voice becomes feeble & unheard

Due to human ploys I become paralyzed
But your smile & gaze make me hypnotized

Give me strength not to fall for these follies
But live each moment as if it's endless jollies

Give me the hope to pass on the message
For which we are part of this entourage

Bless me that I do not lose voice & sight
Let me not enter into any new fight

Let the candle of hope burn forever
Let it be held in reverence forever

For you are my hope and my guide
Without which there wouldn't be a ride

This is a sincere and humble prayer
To shower your divine grace as every year

Lest I might forget what I am here for
And keep asking for more and more

Those things which neither I nor
Anyone should not have asked for

As they do not contribute to the growth
But will be the reason for loath

Let me be a tool in your divine play
Mould me as though I'm a piece of clay

I shall be glad to serve you till
My last breath as per Your will.

My heart is for You

On a cool and breezy morning
I'm lost in the nature's charming
I decided to paint Your glory
With all the details of the story
Took out a beautiful brush
Began to recollect memories afresh.

Time went on & I was lost
Completely covered in frost
I came back to the present
Wishing I could represent
In simple words or colours
Your glorious & wonderful morals.

Slowly, I realized that Your song
Of glory is indeed very long
It is told, retold, sung & re sung
I do not know where to again begun
But I'm determined to search a way
This way I was immersed whole day.

Days passed into nights, but still
I've no clue as to how to fill
The void & emptiness in me
Created out of this search for thee
At last, I jotted down these lines
Couldn't depict Your grace & shines.

But these lines filled the void
I realized that I'm not devoid
Of expression to portray Your brilliance
But there are uncountable millions

Of ways and expressions to praise
I'm just a new born daisy or maize.

Searching for Your divine manifestation
I realized I can only do proper justification
By offering my heart to You Lord of the Lords
Then there wouldn't be a need for words
I shall dedicate my heart & me
For a divine cause to realize thee.

United for a Cause

Mystically separated in union
Divinely united in separation
Spreading divinity across
Pacifying the pain in case of loss
Consoling one another in such times
Completing each others' lines
Forbearing the others flaws
Without any pause or clause
Understanding beyond comprehension
Acceptance beyond apprehension

Arranging meeting for a purpose
Withstanding any kind of blows
Land or sea or earth or heaven
Their grace is unique & divine
Time and distance are never a concern
Their strong bond is beyond any yearn
United for an angelic cause
Prepared for any kind of loss
Their birth & death are a divine play
Passing message to mankind in a gentle way.

Necklace

I started collecting beads for a necklace
Engrossed in this task in a fast pace

Fortunately arrived at multiple colours
Loved them more than any of the flowers

Flowers wane off in a day or two
But my beads are always a pretty view

Permanently glitter my proud possessions
They became a symbol of my assertions

The beads have become my identity
They represent my thirst & vanity

But a day came when I couldn't bear
And stopped suddenly to wear

This piece of pride around my neck
Initially I felt like a piece of wreck

Slowly, I learnt there are many more
Jewels precious than those I adore

Restricting to few lovely beads
Narrowed my vision & deeds

There is always a beauty in re beginning
It is vital evidence that you are living

All my old beads and new jewels now
Filled me with a mystical grace and Love

I took pride now not in wearing these
But in sharing & rejoicing in blissful peace.

Last Moments

When I'm about to reach the other side
Of the Shore which is indeed very wide
I wish you to dwell deep inside me
To give me the moral courage to see
The new shores with wide open eyes
Never lose faith or assume that our vow dies
When my boat is ready for me to board
I pray to you to strike a chord
Accept the situations as is & be bold
Let the future moves of His play unfold
I wish, you whisper sweet nothings
In this physical plane these feelings
Are for the last time, these expressions
Are just like humble confessions
Which I would love to repeat Dear
All through my journey to cast off fear
And they shall be forever imbibed
As our souls are never ever divided
They shall remain together passing on
Divine message though one of us is gone
Merely from the worldly existence
This shall not create any distance
Miles cannot separate our togetherness
It might seem to the world as aloofness
But it is like an interwoven thread
That which is permanently wed
Miraculously for a divine cause
That which is part of Nature's Laws.

Tranquility

On a lovely walk in the garden
When there is nothing to abandon

At that moment when all your possessions
Are distributed and they created impressions

In the hearts and the souls of your mates
You shall now not fall for any of the baits

You are glowing with unknown grace
Now that you are quite a familiar face

To a lonely passerby or a good old friend
Because you are on a mission to send

Across the divine message of the Lord
Good or bad, doesn't affect your chord

You've achieved a state of balance
That which is manifested as brilliance

Your strength that lies in composure
Is a sensible way of divine disclosure

Those surrounded around you experience
Tranquillity beyond material abundance

This is the gift bestowed to one and all
Portrayed by those who follow the divine call.

Mother's Embrace

The warmth in mother's bosom
That which is just like a blossom
Of various unexpressed emotions
Just like one of the divine potions

Lovely comfort and divine embrace
The warmth that which stays for days
In just a few moments of togetherness
The child experiences acceptance and forgiveness

The heavy heart of the child becomes light
Just like an enchanted feather filled with might
The pain passes to the mother from the child
Which the mother accepts in a way that is mild

The child is filled with fresh energy
Ready to go and strike synergy
The mother divinely takes up the pain
So that her child shall never be in vain

She provides comfort and wanes away
Any discomfort in the child's way
She gives the moral strength & courage
For the child to fight any outrage

Tender & blessed is their connection
This reminds one the day of Resurrection
Divine grace is manifested as mother's love
Just not her child but the mystics too shall bow.

Let's discover

I'm a wanderer who is in a quest
Always filled with unknown unrest
Wandering across mountains & plains
In scorching summer or when it rains
Reaching across new people and places
Or am I running away from worldly races?
But there's a joy in keeping on moving
An association similar to winds roaring
When I feel like resting for a while at a place
The place itself starts changing in new ways.

Is change my shadow or my identity?
Or is this one of the ways to reach infinity
I'm not able to comprehend this logic
But what I can do is enjoy this magic
Let the future unfold and unravel
I wish to add co-passengers in this travel
Let this mystified lanes teach me to grow
Let me always stay humble to bow
To the nature's myriad beautiful plays
That shines splendidly on the human race.

Memories

Assets that I can carry till my last breath
That may not be separated even after death
Glorious possessions which eye cannot see
But these hold one's life's treasures key
All my life I have been assimilating them
Because it is one of the priceless gem
That one can carry safely deep inside heart
That which makes you feel apart
From the crowd that surrounds you
Because this is shared only by a few
The people with whom you can share
Such invaluable gems in life bear
You in times of your pain and pleasure
They are indeed your life's treasure
Their support is beyond any measure
It is whole hearted without any seizure
You remain wilfully & solemnly captured
In their humble presence raptured
They are gem like possessions that which
Stay close to your bosom & make you rich
These may be termed as memories
They are immeasurable richest treasuries
People associated with these memories are
Angels in your life shining brightly as a star.

Dear Honey...

You held me tightly and closely
In the moments when I was lonely

You are my source of inspiration
Filling each moment with admiration

At times I haven't expressed my gratitude
Busily craving for higher altitude

As it was you who taught me to aim
And to always burn like a flame

Lightening the world around and
Spreading happiness in the land

My adoration for you is beyond words
As you equipped me with the swords

To fight and make a way in this place
Lest I might have been last in the race

You made me realize amidst worldly chatters
That it is the journey that which matters

In all my life's endeavours and efforts
Your name shall be embossed in golden letters

My expression is not complete yet
I'm at a crossroad searching to get

A chance to express my admiration for you
Journey with you is always unexpected & new

When I shall get such a glorious chance
That moment shall be merry as its divine dance

For I'm always grateful to the Lord
As you are my life's precious reward.

Fragrance

World is filled with many a colours
Multiple shades from variety of flowers
Those grow in our very own garden
Whose blossom relives us from burden
They nurture our thoughts and actions
Enable us to take right steps in transitions

The beauty is- we are our own gardeners
We are blessed to be its defenders
Protecting it from any kind of damage
Nurturing it all through our age
The fragrance of these flowers extends
Even till the last second & never ends

The essence is indeed absorbed forever
In the surroundings & it shall never
Loose its charisma and beauty
Nature takes up it as its duty
To spread the fragrance across
So that there shall never be a loss

Divine and blessed is the one
Who took up the role of a son
Or a daughter to the Mother Earth
It is a journey whose worth
Cannot be expressed in words
Cannot be measured in yards

Let the myriad colours & differences be appreciated
Let us respect the uniqueness & never get divided
Its impact shall divinely be felt by progeny
Through the harmonious homogeny
Left as imprints in the form of fragrance
On the earth which is beyond flagrance.

A Healer

When you talk I could hear
The message to be free from fear
When I grasp the essence of your words
I develop strength to fight any kind of swords
When I hear your gentle mirth
I get lost in appreciating your worth
When I see you in moments of pain
I stop being remorseful and vain
The very passing thought of yours
Makes me open new doors
Gentle doors that let fresh air
That teaches me to learn and care
New doors of thinking have opened
These are very serene & can mend
Even a destructive thought
It gives me the strength to fight
Any kind of irregularities or differences
There's divine beauty in these experiences
I'm yet to be blessed with an expression
To define your imprints & the impression
That you leave back on this land
Without the use of any magical wand
You have the power to heal
The strength to accept & feel
Other's pains & emotions beyond
Expression & can be immersed a pond
Full of emotions and feelings
Adding essence and meanings
To the scattered words & chatter
Adding spirit & soul that really matters.

Door

I opened the door to let in fresh air
To fill the space with warmth & care

The door was just partly opened now
I could feel sunshine, warmth & love

Flowing along with the morning breeze
Making me immobilised and freeze

My heart beat has turned into a rhythm
I was immersed in a lyrical anthem

It made me feel refreshed and light
My ecstasy has reached a new height

I entered a dream like state
Where there is no role for fate

I could hear a gentle whisper of a bird
As if it is a message from the Lord

I could hear the chimes swinging
Widening my thoughts horizon & rising

Reminding me to open the door completely
Let me open it and get lost deeply

It's essential to get lost to find one self
This is like reunion with one's own unknown self.

Stranger in a busy street

On a usual week day in the ever busy lane
When the sky was clear & there's no rain
When each one is lost in their own world
Without time to pay attention to any herald
Rushing from one job to another
Gasping for breath in midst to go further
If not they are scared they might perish
Scared to explore where they'd vanish
Few are aware that all this is not permanent
Yet try to build something which is eminent
In this chase they forget their own identity
Losing track of the path and its serenity
Going after trifles assuming they'd bring eternity
Forgetting the need to form & nurture fraternity
To remind these long last divine deals
An angel entered the street to see & feels
That there is a long way ahead for them to realise
As they do not even see an Angel from Paradise
Has just entered the street as a surprise
They are so busy and thus fail to recognise
That a helping hand has come from far off places
To make them feel bright and have happy faces
The Angel remained a stranger in midst of their chores
Decided to make an impact but without any force
Been patient and helpful to whoever came across
Tried to make them feel better and pacify their loss
Slowly the busy street turned to a happy street
Each one enjoying their job and a new feat
They smiled at strangers and welcomed everyone
With open arms embraced change & had fun
Stopped seeing a new entrant as an enemy but
As a treasure and who could sharpen their wit

They forgot the one who brought this change
This might seem indeed very strange
But this was the Angel's wish and will
That they remember their purpose & stand still.

Crossroads

A traveller has reached a unique crossroad
Split for choice with regard to the mode
To be adopted to keep moving forward
As he felt there is something downward
The downward trend he feels is reflected
In all turnings where in the road deflected

He was slowly loosing the track
His steps slowly lost trail & felt slack
Unable to make proper judgement
Could not find an outlet to vent
He paused for a second, stayed still
Wanted to experience light &re- fill

Fill with fresh and revitalizing powers
Pondered if he was looking for towers?
Towers of power or glory or fame?
Or is he trying to encrypt his name
On each and every possible leaf
Is he filling himself with grief?

For a second he felt enlightenment dawn
He felt like all the burden & pain as gone
He looked at the path he covered till then
The travelled path has made him strengthen
His inner grit and move forward
As there is no point going backward

If he could cover such a long way
He felt a very fresh & strong ray
Of hope- that there is always a chance
To move ahead & have a merry dance

Looking at the path already travelled
He felt a truth has been just unravelled

A timeless truth that there is no reason
To stay behind & wonder when it is our season
Our precious season of blossom to learn
Learn from old mistakes & never feel worn
Hope is the essence of journey of the humanity
It graciously leads us to our destiny.

Silent, Serene Walk

Along with my dear friend I'm walking
On a serene walk which I've been longing
Since many a days but didn't utter
A word, initially it was like a flutter

The road's curves at times dives me deep
Scary, as I started slowly to peep
Deep inside my own identity
Unsure if at all I'm a human entity

The journey took deep & steep turns
Healed many a buried burns
It was a ride of re-discovery
As if it is essential for recovery

It is fulfilment of unexpressed wishes
Filling life with invaluable riches
Making me gently feel lovable
Letting me know that I'm adorable...

Beyond Boundaries

A kid saw the World map once
It was her first look & hence
Got a strange & innocent doubt
That she couldn't answer & sought
Her mother's help for the aspect
As it was beyond her intellect

Her mother took her near
To know what's bothering her dear
The kid enquired innocently why
There are so many lines in map, invisible to the eye
Her mother explained they are boundaries
Separating the different lands & countries

She is neither yet convinced nor seemed agreeable
Why did we draw them when they aren't visible?
Her mother said it's for political & economic reasons
It is not meant to create any sort of treasons
The child looked at her mother perplexed
Her mother understood her concern & reflected

That it is vital not to create any barriers
It is essential & important to be Warriors
Of Hope, faith & Careful Carriers
Of the message of unity & its Saviours
Then no boundaries shall exist
They are just lines of ink covered by mist

That ceases to exist when we stand united
Never even dreaming to be divided
The kid felt convinced and beamed
Happy that what she dreamed

About the world being without borders
Is possible and there are no true dividers

Freedom is indeed a reality
The existence of duality
Is just an illusion of the eye
For which there is no reason to vie
A world without boundaries is indeed
A reality & is dependent on one's deed.

A friend in the nature's walk

On one of the evening walks
To open the self created padlocks

Which make one feel breathless
Dipped in gloom and being hopeless

When the soul repeatedly whispers
That I shouldn't be one of the blisters

There is no purpose of locking
It is gracious to be unlocking

All the self created restrictions
Soaring high beyond distinctions

The gentle breeze elevated my mood
Lifting the gloomy & sorrowful hood

I saw something & I unlocked in this walk
All the dim ideas, it's a beautiful peacock

It took my breath away for a second
This was something I never reckoned

Nature is a great healer and has power
To take away any sort of glower

Let me walk in the heart of the nature
Forever being its companion in the adventure.

Morning Mist

The path was covered with morning mist
The road is partly covered & the twist
Of the lane is not clearly visible
Not allowing one to have a sensible
Decision or judgement about the turn
There is no grace to speed up or run
It's essential to keep moving ahead
To maintain momentum and regard
This as a chance to remain anonymous
To meditate on your own truth & conscious
A passer by assumes you are a stranger
None shall abhor you away, as if a danger
In the lap of nature the mystical morning mist
Is an invisibility cloak, it's not a weed or a cyst.

This mist covers you tenderly for a while
Helps you walk self immersed for a mile
It's not to hide your true identity
But to prepare for a new dawn & reality
When the warm sunshine touches
Your forehead & you're cheek blushes
There is a new opportunity to portray
The mystical light absorbed by the ray
Of the morning sunshine that took away
All the pain you had in a simple sway
Only after experiencing the mist we
Feel blessed to have light and see
The newly born divine dawn
In the path of our lovely lawn.

Awe

In those moment of awe
When you just saw
Something beyond human eyes
Comprehension, wherein lies
The serenity of a life time
Cannot be measured in dime
Difficult to express in words flow
As if some unique feelings sow
You are experiencing divine bliss
That is never worth a miss
An untold charm in your actions
You are filled with serene sensations
That brings in unusual vibrations
You need no one's justifications

It is one of the rare and unique occasions
A joy that cannot fit any definitions
A moment of complete acceptance
Beyond the feeling of Forbearance
A moment of complete surrender
When you are lost to render
An expression to this divinity
When the soul experiences felicity
The dualism of the world seems
Just a facade and one of the names
All the masks covering your eyes
Are removed, there seems to be no vice
The power of the self is beyond imagination
The real 'you' is beyond comprehension!

Silence

In the moments of serenity & silence
One is gifted with the beauty of resilience
The strange and odd ripples created
In the midst of happenings are cleared

The mind is clear out of all confusions
Every idea is bathed in diffusions
Those moments when the whole world
Is fast asleep, but you stay curled

Wide awake to your thought process
You listen to each moment with aptness
Paying more attention and respect
To life's meaning & the prospect

Of finding a treasure deep inside you
That which opens a new view
A very clear view of the scenery
Filling the heart with a sense of victory.

Soothing Words

Words from the heart have unique powers
Soothing like monsoon's first showers
They give you the strength to walk alone
Under the scorching sun without a moan

Make you resilient to the changes around
You discover new light which can surround
Not just yourself but your companions as well
Staying united, where in your heart shall dwell

It takes away the pain away from you
Your life is afresh like a snow dew
But it doesn't melt away easily
Instead leaves its marks diligently.

Bird's Journey

A bird which just learnt how to fly
Was full of energy to soar high
To reach unknown places & discover
The miracles of life and have power
To make a name and earn its identity
To shine beyond any kind of hostility
To discover the essence of its birth
Learn and grow to prove its worth

In this process it set on a journey
Believing it to be its own attorney
In its journey it met new companions
It emerged as one of the best champions
At other times the bird was confused
Lost in the mire but strongly refused
To accept defeat and again soared high
Its goal is to achieve; not scared even to die

In this course, at times it was hurt
At times the injury was in the spirit
That took longer time to heal
This was indeed a messy deal
That which opened wounds hitherto sealed
With an injured spirit the bird kneeled
Before the Altar of the Lord to guide
To give it the strength not to hide

To bestow clarity & determination
His mercy is beyond any limitation
Graciously & gently obliged the prayer
Gave it the strength to fight & forbear
The bird learnt instead of trying to hide

To take pain & pleasure in the same stride
Then life is a walk with the Lord as a companion
There is nothing here to possess or abandon

Life is a flow where there is no need
To pile grudges or let others feed
On one's weakness or to misguide
This is one's own journey to find
Treasures hidden inside one's own self
That can connect this existence to divine self
To do the best with the given resource
Have no fear as there is always Recourse.

Surprise Gifts

Strange aspects that comes in special ways
That when opened fill you with radiant rays

You feel blessed with these presents
You are not aware of their presence

They were very much there deep inside
Awaiting you to open them and confide

The moment the treasure is opened
It is like a surprise gift rediscovered

Your joy knows no bounds
They can heal any kind of wounds

These gifts buried are divine qualities
Forgotten as we are lost in realities

Differences of illusion & reality are blurred
Many painful bruises are carefully cured

If the healer is very much inside you
Why are you searching & losing view?

Strange question with a simple answer
These surprises open up only to empower

When one accepts who he is and vows
Not to manipulate & completely bows

Before the divine will with complete surrender
Enabling harmony and not accepting to asunder.

Path

Out of the multiple paths ahead of him
A wanderer chose a path in random
He didn't apply any kind of logic
But wished it to be full of magic

He started travelling on it joyfully
Had wonderful company initially
He multiplied his speed and raced
His eagerness at times left him dazed

At times he was full of energy
This was when he had synergy
At other times he felt his energy drain
As though he is about to lose breath & wane

But he rebuilt his energy and walked
Curious to meet the end & feel relived
But the path had many twists and turns
He couldn't see the end & the returns

One day he arrived at a crossroad
He looked around & felt bestowed
He felt this can be a chance to re begin
Spent some moments in silence to regain

Composure and clarity to move forward
He learnt life isn't ever measured in yard
It is a collection of rhythms & its patterns
Beautiful assimilation that matters

He started his journey enjoying the solace
That the nature offers and felt flawless
There is no beginning or end to this path
It is the depth that matters, but it is not math!

Divine Expressions

We talk to be heard or to be understood
Or to lighten ourselves when bored
Or to express deepest of our emotions
Or share the little & fragile confessions?

It can be a combination of any feelings
It is a way of opening wrappings
Of many unknown gifts that lie
Behind silence not ready to die

How do these serene gifts appear?
Are they born to disappear?
Strangely these gifts are born
In the moments when we are torn

At the times when we are low
When there is an inner row
The best of our true self emerges
When our consciousness submerges

When we drift swiftly in infinity
Forgetting our existence or affinity
To worldly moments & divisions
This is when we discover our visions

When we are lost in a sea of thought
Not even aware what is that brought
This moment of rejoice and rhyme
That made us even forget to look at time

We feel a connection with ourselves
There is no division into halves
Our existence discovers a purpose
When we blossom afresh like a rose

This moment of serenity is to be cherished
It is a glorious moment to be worshipped
As it discovered significance of your existence
It bridged the heart's & brain's distance!

It is your choice to express these feelings
In words or deeds to emphasize meanings
But one cannot expect to be understood
Cannot be used to lighten up when bored

It's a precious deed to express our emotions
Cannot be equated to sharing or confessions
These expressions are to be painted
So that they remain forever imprinted

Imprinted forever on this lovely land
For our progeny to appreciate this sand
To believe that there is a helping hand
That, harmonious growth is a magical wand.

Divine Dawn

At the moments when night passes into day
As though a woman lifting her veil in a way
That is gradual & filling surroundings with light
Fears are casted off slowly, spreading might
Taking away all illogical ignorance & fear
Giving us the courage to come very near
To our own true self which was clouded
Buried in veils of disguise & never moulded
To manifest our inner charisma and glow
Lifting of the veil of ignorance lets a flow
Of words and expressions wrapped till date
Deep inside the bosom & letting fate
Play to the tunes of mysterious lyrics
Rising the mood of our sleeping spirits
To unknown rhythms & tunes
Making us discover new runes
Elevating our presence to new heights
Where there is no place for dark nights
This is the breaking of a new dawn
Enabling the sunlight to fall on the lawn
Of dark & grey shades to erase their impact
Silently & gracefully entering into a new pact
Wherein we agree to greet the warm sunshine
With open arms & smiles each day, as it is divine.

Untold Tale of Self

Days passed into dark nights
Nights into months, but the fights
Fought deep inside my heart
Have never stopped their wrath

At times I felt broken into pieces
Felt life is a gamble or a game of dices
Searched for the balm to relieve
So that I can learn, grow and relive

I've been wandering soul less
On this planet to get out of this mess
Encountered people who are immersed
In the worldly pleasures and drenched

Absorbed in the glory of timeless victories
Tried to learn from their success stories
But Alas, I couldn't walk in their path
I continued to carry even more wrath

Came across people who are blissful
Contented in life's journey & wishful
This made me stop & think for a while
I pondered over what brought that smile

The bliss on a child's face without any effort
Which is very peaceful and has a comfort
That is difficult to define in any terms
That breaks all conventional norms

The answer for which I'm wandering
Is present in complete surrendering
To the divine call without any queries
It is the magic that relieves all worries

The divine call is heard when one
Has complete faith such that none
Could deviate you from your chosen ideals
As life is not a combination of deals

It is a journey of walking ahead
So that your tale doesn't go unsaid
Dark nights are followed by bright dawn
Freshness replaces the feeling of worn.

Thoughts

Certain thoughts rejuvenate your soul
Few beliefs make you complete & whole
World's chatter & opinions at times make
You split and torn in heart for the sake
Of ideals that you may never understand
But you try to go with them to be in the land
You forget your identity in this game
But feel contended that you have a name
Achieved your goals & have fame
As time passes you start feeling lame

When you go back down memory lane
Search for moments when you were sane
You find it difficult to identify yourself
You catch only few glimpses of yourself
Those are the moments when you
Immersed yourself in the view
Not concentrating on your personal gain
But helping others who are in pain
You couldn't identify with things like
Name or fame for which you did all hike

Shouldn't we enter the race for winning?
Or should we cease altogether running?
Ceasing to do things brings hopelessness
It will kill your instinct & distinctiveness
There is serenity in keeping on moving
Imbibing the beauty of surrounding
Filling with thoughts that rejuvenate the soul
To enable one to feel complete and whole
Bringing solace by adding rhythm to the tunes
Of life with messages from surrounding views

The results of our actions are not ours
They are the response of destiny's hours
Hours of effort and hard work for food
Intended for the welfare & greater good
Of not just you, but those around you
Who believe in you & live for you
Life is a collection of lessons told & retold
That teach, let us grow wise and old
Why can't we picture our entire life
With such beautiful images in rife?

Your existence

I've been searching for you
Without limiting my view

I have no proofs of your identity
To bring back me to my sanity

My song of your praise has been
Going on & on but you are unseen

I couldn't meet you in the new land
Nor did I find you in the desert sand

I searched for you in the fresh water
Where there is no human slaughter

I tried to see your name in high skies
Where there are no silly vies

You are there in every fresh breath
I take, this shall continue till death

I cannot forget your fire like passions
Your aims are beyond building mansions

In my search for you, I've discovered
Many a fairy tale like realities, indeed

But my search is not yet complete
Now, I don't find any other way for this feat

I request you to guide me from here
As I'm clueless as to where you are there

Let this journey have a meeting place
This shan't be forgotten in this race

This is my prayer, quite humble & deep
It'll be treasured as a gift & shall keep

It in the deepest layers of my heart
As it'll be my existence, not just a part!

Striking Sky

The leaves are curiously fluttering
Trying to reveal mysteries & uttering

That this is a blessed monsoon
This is the time to rejoice & soon

Drench oneself in the rain of love
Come let's sing squeaked the dove

But it wasn't visible to the eye
Searching for it, reached mountain high

Looked above & was amazed at what lie
Above the highest view, it's the striking sky

Filled with fresh & wonderful emotions
Ready to down pour in large portions

The view is beyond words description
It is the Lord's signature & encryption.

Rising from ruins

Just like the flute's pacifying tunes
My soul is rising from ruins

It's been buried there since ages
Waiting for some mystical sages

Miraculous water to cleanse
To dig deep & demonstrate it's dense

The tunes may not make sense
To a passerby, but to know it's essence

It is imperative to turn the heart
Into a string that knows the art

Of playing to the tunes of unspoken words
To recover from the bruises of sharp swords

Unspoken words & promises carry
A deeper significance which never vary

There's pre set harmony in these tunes
That is making my heart rise from ruins.

Delusions

In the pitch darkness at mid night
When nothing caught one's sight
Searching for things through touch
Came across an article on the couch

Didn't recognize nor feel what it is
Tried to search my memory not to miss
But to record the strange sensation
It's touch is soothing unlike an invasion

Couldn't emote to express the feel
But it was trying to mysteriously heal
In between the lungs there was a hollow
Tried to pick the thing to swallow

But it fit well in between the lungs
Felt that this is the strange songs
Unsung lyrics lying on the couch
When the brain is busy to vouch

Brain buried in events around us
Getting lost in the worldly fuss
The pitch dark is replaced by light
Fresh & bright ready for any fight

This bright light filled with fresh hope
Taught not to tie oneself with rope
This is the time to act & cope
Never try to patch up or mope

Destroys the hollow not just inside me
But anyone who comes to see
Their identity from among the debris
And tries to fill the void with merries

This is the moment to remove delusions
Rise against self created illusions
Rise above what your hood can sway
You are the hope and beam of ray!

You

Your arrival is marked with newness
It brought wonderful freshness
I'm delighted to be in your presence
It is bringing me back to my senses

This a new dawn in my existence
This is filling unknown distance
I seem to come closer to my own self
Stopped defining to the world myself

This is the delight of knowing you
How else would it taste if I realize you?
This feeling of delight to be in this dream
Let this be the ultimate truth in my realm

To be born afresh & anew each day
Not to bow to the worldly chatter or say
To stay allied with authenticity in my own self
I bow to Your will & completely offer myself

In this moment of confessions
Let me make small disclosures
This may seem more of a question
Than an answer to the assertion

When I was with strange queries
Presumed to be buried in worries
Why didn't I stop the self imposed cruelty
Have faith in the assertion that you are the reality?

Time heals & has answers, as this is a process
Let me not walk back into my previous mess
Let the freshness of a new born flower
That which just erupted in me not glower

Let the delight of knowing your existence
Be wrapped warmly & blur all distance
If this is the delight of knowing you
How else would it taste if I realize you?

Beacon

A shiny object is serving as a beacon
Its light is to strengthen or weaken?
Only time can define this destiny
Sweet or sour this fruit of reality
It is definitely a unique walk
Filling the path with many a rock

The beacon is up on a tower
This long walk is for power
Or is it for a fragrant flower?
Should this walk be slower?
Is there any need to walk at all?
The gentle voice heard is the call

As the call is heard & the path chosen
There is no necessity to loosen
One's belt that has been buckled
There's no need to be dazzled
It is just one of the many paths
You shall not carry any wraths

It is to empty your burdens
Not to build any fences
Do not judge the path or the walk
Just walk the path as if it is a talk
A talk with your own self to move
It is just to keep the pace & hove

Let the moments just pass on
For nothing is pain to moan
Let the light of the beacon cool

It is your own reflection in a pool
A pool of gracious gifts to be unwrapped
Those which are very delicately draped

Adorned in the voices of the world around
It is your own self that will surround
The shiny object called beacon
Is not to strengthen or weaken
It is to discover your identity
To enable you to immerse in eternity.

Musings

Strange musings are heard & felt
It made the heart magically melt

The musings dug very deep
The heart started to weep

It flooded not with tears
But cut open deep rooted fears

Wrapped deep inside for ages
It is a combination of rages

This musing has a mystical glow
That can make any emotion flow

Once the flow of fears ceased
It was very soothing & eased

Not just the untold pain & vain
But the hidden bruises & slain

It's rebirth after a thousand deaths
Regaining energy & lost breaths

To gain balance & composure
To enjoy the ride of self disclosure

Strange musings are heard & felt
It made the heart magically melt!

A walk

Began a walk across a freshly
Mown grass that's precisely
Shaped & grown by the gardener
To give a look that is cleaner

Many tools helped the process
To grow & mown this grass
Each step brought calmness
Filling unrevealed emptiness

Foot that touched the land
Felt support of an invisible hand
The walk gave unknown gifts
It helped cross many rifts

It taught the art of compassion
It revived long lost passion
A passion for living at the moment
To follow the heart & ascent

Climb the stairs of glory to heaven
To reach the stars & deepen
The bonds of love invisible
To the naked eye but sensible

To live and dedicated one's life
Without getting lost in the strife
This is the whisper of the breeze
To stay connected & not to freeze

Usha Nandigama

Connected to the holy abode
This is a wonderful road
Carved by beautiful hands
With love & care not wands.

Dark Alley

Walked down the deepest & dark alley
Desperately wishing to see a flower valley

But was greeted with warm sunshine
The warmth brought surprise yet was fine

Newness made eyes twinkle in awe
It's a gracious surprise, what I just saw

It's beyond human contention
All the nerves became numb & the intention

For its arrival is marked with queerness
Been waiting for this warmth with eagerness

Never expected to meet it at this alley
The scene around is no more a valley

It looked as if paintings from a museum
I became a curator in this museum

Next second it looked like a theatre
I'm a character in a play in this theatre

Later it looked like a dense forest
I look like a tribe's inhabitant in this forest

I gained composure after a while
There is all bliss and only smile

These curious paintings & imaginations
Ceased for a while & reached conclusions

Everything kept changing in the green space
But my emotion was never lost in the race

This is the gift I received walking
Down the dark alley as if lurking

Next time I go through this lane again
I shall not ponder but let it flow & wane.

A song

You are present in all my dreams
You are the Lord of my realms

My presence didn't leave a mark
But your love replaced light with dark

My blabbering became ornaments of words
My companions started repeating these words

It is your elegance that they sing
It deepens my adoration & shall ring

The fact that I'm still alive
To recite your greatness & dive

Deep into meditative trance
To sing your glory & dance!

Springing of Hope

In the midst of summer I felt cold shivers
It was the flow of unexpressed emotional rivers
They have flown crossing the barriers
Became the voice of representative carriers

Not just of my lost identity and self
But the mark of freedom and myself
Then came the fresh blossom of spring
My soul danced & heard bells ring

The bells sang in the chorus
To brighten and awaken us
From the confused expression of interjection
Filled with feelings of resentment & rejection

The bells sang in a glorious harmony
It is the celebration of birth ceremony
Of not a baby or a bird, but hope
It is the spring morning's birth of hope!

New Glory

Eyes are searching for light
Heart wants to be filled with might
Hands are searching for company
Breath is waiting for symphony
Soul is searching for solace
Sense is warning about a mace
Dived deep to watch the turbulence
It was dark inside but made no sense
Senses lost their feel & became numb
Voice shivered & became dumb.

It was a moment filled with despair
The heart is broken without repair
Tried to join the broken pieces
They appeared to be flying dices
With no option & chance to rescue
The bleeding heart was left in dew
A lightning bolt struck the vicinity
Everything became lively in infinity
The feeling of numbness is lost
There is no pain or scar in this frost.

For a moment it appeared worst
But later realized this is the most
Lively moment the heart was waiting
It is the breaking of fears & rising
To a new dawn & to a new toast
The truth is the heart is never a roast
It just needed some time to heal
To re-live past injuries & reel
Brighten up from lost glories
To create new miracles & glories.

Peace

Brought together limestone & sand
To build an abode in this land

Where your name is a celebration
People immerse in your divine sensation

I walked place to place to search
For a beautiful location, tried to reach

A land which will help me to hold
Not just an idol of yours but unfold

Your mysterious nature and divine play
To spend in solace the rest of the day

After daily toil & regular monotony
To cast off the feeling of lethargy

In this journey I went to new lands
Thought about you & left in the hands

Of the people the choice to build
A castle, for their hearts to be ruled

Forever & ever through this synchrony
They enjoyed the solitude & left dichotomy

Each one built a temple not in any art
But sacredly very deep inside their heart

Ready to share and embrace it
My deepest desire has graciously lit

The sense of hope in my companions
My soul is now devoid of delusions

I shall rest forever in peace now
As each step is filled with your love.

Inspiration

A chirping bird travelled long way
It was a long & sunny tiresome day

Day was passing into dusk
The sky is wearing a new mask

The bird started its journey back home
A nest wherein its babies waits for her to come

Suddenly she lost track of its usual path
Lost in some scary thought & filled in wrath

It became quite dark & the bird felt
Trapped in the darkness & wept

She had no choice but to stay in a furrow
Worrying about the babies & in sorrow

She didn't blink its eyes & at the first
Sight of the dawn gave a halt to the rest

Began its onward journey towards home
She prayed to see her babies safe at home

Finally reached its nest and to her dismay
Found the nest to be empty without even hay

She squeaked & searched for them desperately
She started feeling remorse & very insanely

Lost all hope & sat in deep pain
The sky was cloudy & it started to rain

After the rain halted & the sky is clear
She heard chirping; to her it's very dear

It was her dear ones voice she felt
Experienced hell at the thought & wept

Her eyes couldn't believe the sight
Her younger ones are coming from right
She thanked the Lord & her heart swell
Surprised to see how they could fly so well

The younger ones took the step to fly
To protect themselves & not to fall prey

To a predator that tried to kill
They forgot that they can't fly well

Their only strength at the moment was
Their mother's love & it became a cause

Not just to safeguard them against foe
A sense of inspiration & an end to row.

Usha Nandigama

Lifting of Veil

Gentle breeze is flowing eastward
It is lifting the veil & making it hard
To repress any kind of unspoken words
It is striking a deep chord in the yards
Of the heart which is now transforming
Into a beautiful flower & shining

With the lustre of self realization
It's not a usual feeling but a sensation
That is tearing the heart apart
There is a strange & slow depart
Of feelings of guilt & resentment
Its place is filled with contentment

The veil flew off & now it appears
There is ample space not for tears
But to fill heart & soul with cheers
To walk in the path without fears
By removing the veils of limitations
Learning with open mind at all destinations.

Scion

Searched for light in a dungeon
Startled by the presence of a scion
My scion doesn't hail from nobility
Not born or brought up in aristocracy

Has the qualities of a warrior
Decided to be always a Saviour
Followed instincts till the last breath
Left traces & marks after death

These marks are my memories
These traces are my treasuries
I've worn them as shining amulets
That makes me flow like rivulets

I do not have a portrait of yours
To show to the world that clears
The myth that you are imaginary
You are a grand scion & a legendary

I'm an amateur who cannot paint your glory
Nor can I showcase or portray your story
Yet, I know the truth that you are there
You could quench the thirst of my quest in this fair.

Blessed is the soul who could accompany you
As in your company everything presents in a new view
I believe, on one fine day this numbness turns to sensations
The mystery shall be beyond any language's depictions.

Till the moment I'm blessed with your presence
I shall recount your sojourn & immerse in your essence
You shall always stay in the deepest of my heart's closet
You are the invaluable jewel & my heart's rosette!

Glow

In this infinite universe
Let us together find a verse

That is just not an ordinary pattern
Or rhythm but that serves as a lantern

A glowing light emerges from here
Spreading its message to those who dare

To live beyond self created limitations
To cross barriers and all generalisations

This glow is the light of our very own soul
Whose purpose transcends globe & its glow

Has a purpose not just to enlighten
To bring harmony and brighten

Each passing moment of the soul
Makes one feel balanced & whole.

Your charisma

I could feel the fragrance of fresh air
Each time I remembered your flair

I was lost for words when I could hear
The distant whisper to overcome my fears

At times I lost myself in worldly matter
At other times I appeared to be an aberrant

Neither my search nor my journey ended
But I realized it indeed began to send

Not just messages but to meditate
On the glorious life of yours & radiate

A part of the glow around in this sojourn
To enlighten from ignorance & be a soldier

To ward off the fears in this existence
To march forward towards destination

With a deep rooted hope & symphony
Such that this sojourn blesses your company

As it is your charisma which helped surface
These divine qualities by removing all haze.

Anew

A sense of light & anew fulfillment
Moving away from past resentment

Striding across unknown & unseen
Mysterious lanes of rhythmic reign

Leading to a sense of nearing the goal
Manifesting in clear terms one's role

Making one feel complete and whole
Speaking in the language of the soul

Words and signs are carrying new
Meaning & significance to the view

Let this journey mark a period of glory
Let this mark uniqueness in the story

The story that began on the Christmas Eve
Let this journey ensure to leave

An undeniable mark in this life
Let life be viewed from this rife

For life is a beautiful progression
It is not meant to be a transgression

Let divine angels guide in this voyage
Let this message be crossed across ages!

Your Guidance

I carry with me the rare gifts showered
Those which You've graciously bestowed

These are the light for me in dark moments
At times counted as my achievements

They are neither my accolades nor
Do they define who I am in any war

These are neither my life's sole identity
Nor do they fill me with feelings of superiority

These gifts are the humbleness
You taught by depicting kindness

Being patient in times of hardships
Not being slave to any ploys or whips

Striking the chord at the right time
Embracing friends & foes with same rhyme

You've fulfilled your celestial role here
Left it to us to learn to love and care

Your presence on earth is divine delight
It is an infinite & eternal spread of light

Your journey fills one heart with might
Each recounted event is a new height

When one is blessed with Your guidance
Each moment is filled with reverence

This is the greatest gift ever given
Blessed are the souls who've taken!

New Attire

The silence is draped in new attire
It seemed to the world a satire
But is a new born identity & image
With the burial of old rusty cage
To shine brightly like a sage
To leave behind all the rage
Ready to weep to let go of all pain
Intending to cut a part of it & slain
In order to be reborn in new form
Without any intention to sworn

Nature is the witness to this growth
Untainted soul is the taker of oath
Dead to be reborn again from ashes
The past is appearing as if flashes
Assimilation of all the pain & pleasure
The journey ahead is to find a treasure
It is a combination of all knowledge
Learnt & passed on to bridge
The gap between the heart and brain
This is present not to erode or wane

Life is a marvellous transformation
It is gracious to be lost in this sensation
To cherish each second as a gift
Make it valuable by reducing rift
To believe each day is a treasure's jewel
It seems to be a violent upheaval
But the jewel's beauty is disclosed
When all confusions are diffused
A fresh realization shall dawn
Now, silence's new attire is draped on!

A tale to unveil

Embrace yourself & your unique nature
It is a way to discover divine nature

Journey into one's own self is a sensation
A mystical way to see your own reflection

A reflection which was wrapped deep
That which naked eye cannot peep

Discovering your own nature is a ride
Filled with unwrapping of many a hide

This discovery is not devoid of surprise
It lets you walk along the path of sunrise

You are not lost in the crowd
Your presence is your sword

Your identity is presented in your words
You can set synchrony & set chords

The journey is to weave your own tale
Not yet seen or written yet to unveil.

Golden Sword

If you strike me really hard
I shall get up with a golden sword
If you destroy or doom me to death
Beware I shan't pass away in a breath
This is not to prove nor seek vengeance
My golden sword is made of transcendence
It is way beyond your grasp
You shall be left with nothing to clasp
This is a mark of my true self's existence
It shall be embossed in beautiful brilliance

A loyal & truly charming light
That which is beyond your height
It cannot be destroyed in any way
This is my tenderness & also my ray
It shall be a ray of hope for others
Whoever perceives or ever bothers
I was never destined to doom
I shall rise from my ashes to bloom
My golden sword is invisible
Just like my soul it is invincible

You rejoiced once that you've struck
Me a death blow but it was my luck
Luckily, I realized my true identity
Now, I shall reply you with infinity
The source of power for this universe
Shall find a suitable pattern & verse
That can reply you in your language
I'm just a tool not absorbing any rage
I was gifted with invincible sword
To give me courage, protect & guard!

Universal Dream

You are my adorable dream
The purpose of entering this realm
Without which my very existence
Would have been a numb sense
A mere question mark to ponder
If at all, someone tries to wonder.

You are the nectar that fills
The emptiness in barren hills
You are the fragrance that shall bring
Smiles on the faces & makes us sing
You are the ultimate joy & purpose
The reason for millions to rise

You are the inspiration that carries
The universal message of fairies
You are the incarnation of divinity
Enabling us to experience infinity
You are the destiny which we aim
But at times forget in search for name.

You are the joy that fills hearts
The support in times of wraths
You are the inspiration to human race
To lead life in a lively way not as a race
You are the testimony to the fact
That we are part of a divine act.

You are humble not to portray yourself
But we shall rise to raise our own self
You are the Light of Hope

That helps us to get up & cope
You are our support & Guide
We shall always feel by our side.

You are what words cannot grasp
We shall not try to restrict or clasp
You are the seasons that change
To bless us with variety & wide range
You are the flowing water of the rivers
That teaches to keep moving & be drivers.

You are the mountain that stands still
Giving us courage to face any drill
You are the early morning sun shine
That is a message not to whine
You are the warm dusk in the evening
Making us to re-live & relieve in a swing.

You are the faith in man kind
That which reminds us to be kind
You are the new born baby smiling
Ready to reach stars & keep soaring
You are the dream I dream every day
But words cannot describe nor say.

Your manifestation is the ultimate reality
Truth that shall resonate with sensibility
The world with infinite mighty qualities
To overcome dissimilarities & inequalities
To live and let live is the philosophy
Simple yet profound message for synchrony!

New Shores

When the moments of fear cross
Your gates of guts feel like dross
You are not able to leap forward
You question if you are a coward

You know that you are not scared
But you are confused and worried
The thought of leaving the known
Safe harbour doesn't seem sane

You feel to extend & stretch
Yourself in this know wretch
But not experiment in new shores
You weigh pros & cons for hours

Ultimately it's your gut feeling
That rises beyond any dealing
You just leap forward in a second
Strangely your fear is now disband

You yourself are amazed at your
New speed and zeal at the new door
New opportunities lie ahead here
Awaiting your warm welcome there

You keep moving forward with zest
But this leap is never to settle or rest
New shores keep calling you dear
Move ahead gently without any fear!

New Vision

My vision was blocked for a while
I felt as if I'm wandering in an isle
Later my blurred vision is clarified
All around me appeared mystified

Did I ever not notice their presence?
Was I lost in a deep slumber of sense?
Or is it the gift for escaping worldly vision
I felt I'm experiencing a very new season

A season which I never knew existed
It made me dive deep & feel excited
It is a new feeling filled with unfamiliarity
Yet there is a sense of unknown similarity

There is a sense of loosing oneself
Diving deep discovering a new self
Is this re-discovery or self -discovery?
Time alone can uncover this mystery

Let this journey be cherished always
As fresh as the morning sun rays
Let all emotions & feelings be absorbed
To sing a hymn in the name of the Lord

The Christmas Morning is the beginning
Diving in admiration from then & singing
Your hymns all through the day & night
As you are my guide, hope & Knight!

Kingdom of Heaven

I started a beautiful journey ahead
It was mysteriously new & unsaid

Was part of a beautiful garden to play
To learn lessons all through the day

To rest peacefully in the night at shade
With bountiful bliss that can never fade

Ascended stairs at times that are spiral
At times scared of the trips & turns felt viral

But Your grace replaced fear with might
Everything around me seemed right

As what I was embracing was Your grace
I'm no more part of any routine race

Blessed to see Your presence everywhere
To feel Your divine warmth & care

In this Kingdom of Heaven full of Your love
Let me share Your grace around me now

On this Kingdom of Heaven called Earth
Bless me to spread peace & reduce wrath!

Peace – An Identity

I wish the world to be a more peaceful place
Where humanity is not a mask but our face

Wherein our identity is not measured
The differences in races are treasured

Where we speak our heart & we work
For the betterment & not for a perk

Where in lies the greater good of the world
Let this part of human existence not be blurred

A world wherein the primary identity is peace
Where all the turmoil & war shall cease!

Burnt but Learnt

I carried the brunt of your weight
For no mistake of mine & lost sight

Your spiteful nature weakened me
Your vile intentions poisoned me

But you could not destroy me any day
As I'm made of an indestructible ray

You didn't strike me once with a dagger
But dug holes time & again in a swagger

At times, I lost sight of my own path
But never went astray in your wrath

You assumed that I was completely burnt
But the truth is I've risen & learnt

Today I declare to the world with pride
That I've grown stronger with your snide

This is an important lesson for me to learn
It gives one the courage to not to yearn

And fall prey to external forces of manipulation
To look beyond the mask & identify deception

Gave me insight to take note of vile nature
The obnoxious behaviour of such creature

I shall not come after you to seek vengeance
As I shall not waste my energy or intelligence

I believe that the Lord shall teach
That moment I would like to reach

The Creator & thank for the benevolence
The True Power for which my reverence

Is beyond description in any words
That strength shall be stronger than swords

It shall be more powerful & piercing
Than the dagger's wound & more fierce

Than the brutal strength you chose to inflict
Not just on me but many souls like a convict

The moment when you realise you are a Loser
The team of insurgency shall be on a Cruiser!!

Closed Eyes

I closed my eyes & thought the world is dark
Filled full of vile ideas of Bat, jackal & shark

Felt breathless that this is not my place
I thought I shall accept defeat in this race

That I can rest forever in His palm in peace
Suddenly a fresh feeling embraced just like breeze

For the first time I stopped feeling like leaves
That were feeling immense pain & that grieves

As a torn apart wanderer soul on this alien land
I wished to be covered completely by sand

But along the falling leaves of autumn
My fear & hopelessness were also forgotten

The fresh breeze evoke new hopes & dreams
It was the spring time to travel to new realms

It is the time to rise & spring to action
Leaving behind worry, fear & all inaction

My insides gained strength & new voice
I realized I forgot my usual nature to rejoice

I started singing to the tunes of His play
My soul gained serenity in this new ray

I dived deep into this mystical & new shore
Where in lies the essence & purpose of the core

The core strength that created the universe
With all its queerness, beauty & also difference

My closed eyes no more felt it to be dark
It is replaced by a new sense & a new mark

A mark that shall be forever imprinted on me
To reach His abode & blessed to see

His great messages on this lovely planet
With strength to bear the strike of a bayonet

My closed eyes opened to new shores
It is the gateway to opening new doors

New doors of strength, serenity & hope
Expanding the horizons & increasing the scope!

His Painting

What should I talk about the one who is Omnipresent?
How can I describe His myriad surprises & presents?

Who am I to talk about His Omnipresence?
That which is felt in each breath in true essence

How can I glorify His nature which is Omnipotent?
The mystical ways His power manifests & its intent

How can I put in words His benevolence?
That which removes my confusions & ignorance

I can describe neither His Power nor His Grace
I can only sing His already sung glory on all days

That blesses me with new insights on this land
This land is a beautiful painting of His hand

Let us preserve & glorify the land's natural beauty
It shall bestow us to grow & rise for everyday duty!

Tunes from Ruins

A gentle & familiar clasp on my shoulder
To be calm and at the same time bolder

Learn the mysterious splendour of silence
That resonates relaxingly with resilience

To feel the gentle & untainted warmth
In the chilling cold wind on earth

That wind which at times blows you off
It might shake your roots and cast off

Some silly inhibitions or deep rooted fears
Without any tool or taint or any smears

It lets you dance decorously to the tunes
Of the tones that were in buried ruins

The tunes & tones deep inside your heart
Resting there as if an archived art

But alas it is not ruins of a closet
It is destination, quite exquisite & finest

A gentle & familiar clasp on my shoulder
Changed me from a critic to a beholder

Started swirl of the voices buried deep inside
There is no necessity anymore to hide

For this is a journey to create an identity
Weave beautifully a tale of unity & liberty.

A thread

I was part of a routine race
Entered a mysterious maze
Passed time & many a days
Encountered various ways
At times lost vision & sight
Tough times taught might
Lost the track of my path
Filled with unknown wrath.

One day arrived at a crossroads
Each road has light in loads
The light brightened the thought
Any road that shall be sought
Will lead to the destination
This is a unique sensation
As there is no more confusion
All fears are in a state of diffusion.

This state of calmness is beyond
My comprehension & there is a bond
That which connects me to infinity
Is this a unique thread called divinity?
A distinctive thread imbibing affinity
A special connection teaching sensibility
A sense of familiarity to the unknown
Or a part of me which I never owned?

Déjà vu

This is a new and an unfamiliar track
But it strangely pulls me abruptly back
A feeling of unexplainable familiarity
Though there is visible dissimilarity

I sense a bit but gradually loose something
This slowly drives me into a feeling of nothing
I pray humbly for Faith, Strength and Guidance
To guide, as to what has to be trusted in abundance

For my fears are quite deep rooted
Scared as may leave me in mire wrong footed
Fears erupted not in a matter of months or days
But it's been since ages, my heart so says

My heart with an unknown intensity
Immerses in infinity with incredulity instantly
Making me behave in a tender way
To brighten myself up and follow a ray

A ray which mystically guides on any day
It aesthetically arranges life in an array
Is this the sensation called déjà vu?
That shakes ones base & can even blew

Stir innermost deep rooted feelings
Without any agreements or dealings
That leaves you in a state of trance
That lets your soul serenely dance!

Torch Bearers

Passing by the Beautiful Lane
Devoid of Insanity and any Pain
Filled with aroma of perfume
Dancing to a Divine Tune

This is indeed paradise
Where everyone is Wise
The Place of Sun Rise
Hope, Love and Praise

Often viewed as a celestial event
There is no fury or anger to vent
All the senses are Calm and still
But not yet strangely lost and idle

It is the first bloom of freshness
That fills the heart with innocence
Words fail to describe the essence
Pictures fail to paint the credence

Unique sensations run across veins
Yet do not make any untoward claims
Beyond any usual experience
It fills one with unusual indifference

Teaches Oneness and there is no Duality
Helps us to perceive the New Reality
With a unique ability bestowed on us
This is indeed a day of Eternal Bliss

Leading a life of essence on this planet
Till the horizon falls & marked as sunset
Let us feel the warmth of sun till that day
When Human body can sense the divine ray

Let this knowledge make all brave & wise
Enabling them to follow the path of Sun Rise
These Warriors are the torch bearers
They are the Angels walking as saviours!

We

A part of me is always with you
Glowing like a fresh drop of dew
Singing mystically in a sway
Radiating tender beams of ray

Smiling in a serene & silent way
The memory of which makes my day
A worthwhile effort to arise and awake
Filling all void with the serenity of a lake

The lake's water is pure & ever flowing
I'm just a boat which tries to keep rowing
In the depth & warmth of your sea
Sea of emotions in which I cannot see

But feel your presence every moment
It's a proof of your identity as your scent
Reaches the core of my heart & cuts deep
Unspoken pain & it lets me peep

Into my deepest treasures and fears
You enable to gently remove the scars
Without even leaving a mark of the bruise
Lifting my spirits and setting me on a cruise

To progress forward in a journey of light
You are my guidance & the reason for my might
I'm setting on a journey of unknown insights
You are the pillar of support in these heights

Unspoken and untainted words of my soul
Is the pure gift I can offer you as a whole
Not just for being my support or Angel all time
But for transforming my prattle into a hymn

Let me trek forward in this unknown land
I shall see you in each & every grain of sand
I can feel your warm embrace & your hand
That guides me as if a mystical wand

Let this journey be complete with you
Blessing your presence in a rare view
Let me then not be just a dew drop in you
I would love to lose myself forever in you

My body, mind and soul shall feel
Complete at that moment which can heal
Not just all pain, highs-lows & endurance
As it is an unsung journey of assurance

Till then a part of me shall always be with you
Glowing like a fresh drop of dew
Singing mystically in a sway
Radiating tender beams of ray

Smiling in a serene & silent way
The memory of which makes my day
This shall awaken me from the delusion
Destroying fears & filling void with vision!

Crossing bridges

In a state of dizziness I walked alone a mile
The path bestowed both a tear and a smile
Crossed a bridge that had water underneath
Fresh airs touched the forehead in this heath
Gentle breeze woke me up from sleep
Making me feel relief in the deep

The sounds woke up unknown & unfelt energies
After a long time I embraced silence & synergies
Though I walked the mile lone in anguish
I longed to reach the end and make a wish
Setting aside the inner chatter going on forever
I blamed and prayed the Nature for a favour

Then a thought made me think
If I am acting on some brink
Rushing the most memorable journey
Caught up in some unknown spree
Would this trip end in harmony & peace
Or leave me confused & at unease

If I concentrated on the pace of the race
And have not appreciated Nature's Grace
Or preserved the pristine moments of each day
And kept collecting mementos on the way
Would this journey that began in the mother's womb
Bring peace when it ends on a fine moment in the tomb?

What is counted in this sojourn is not the pace
It is the quality of the life & the rest is all haze
Lets not be lost in the mythical amazing maze

But be awake welcoming the days without daze
For the Bridge shall have an impact
Lure the coming generations to act

Guiding them to take the path of bright light
And enlighten them to an unknown great height
This Walk will be memorable to recount
Nurturing the dreams of poets without doubt
That the voyage be profound and possible
Aspiring to achieve even the impossible!

Anonymity

You are the mystical painting that each painter
Paints within self, for which there is no counter

You are the rhythm and verse of any short poem
The meaning & essence of which is indeed an emblem

You are the ground that brings solace and reminds reality
You are the key that reminds to aim high & contain creativity

You are the unknown journey undertaken by humanity
That shall serve as message that the best quality is humility

You are the fragrance of the fresh and new hope that springs
In the hearts of the warrior to fly with noble wishes as wings

You are the potter, painter, poet, philosopher and indeed all
But you still remain anonymous for those awaiting your call

Your anonymity & mysterious play will not bring to stand still
The search to see & listen to your words, as this is our Will.